TURNING NATURAL EDGE BOWLS

BERNARD HOHLFELD

Schiffer Publishing Ltd®

4880 Lower Valley Road · Atglen, Pennsylvania 19310

Other Schiffer Books on Related Subjects:
Segmented Wood Turning. William Smith. ISBN: 076431601X. $14.95
Turning Goblets. Mike Cripps. ISBN: 0764300334. $12.95
Useful Beauty: Turning Practical Items on a Wood Lathe. Dick Sing. ISBN: 0887408516. $12.95
Wood Turning, from Tree to Table: Bowls, Lamps, & Other Projects. Bill Bowers. ISBN: 9780764333354. $16.99

Schiffer Books are available at special discounts for bulk purchases for sales promotions or premiums. Special editions, including personalized covers, corporate imprints, and excerpts can be created in large quantities for special needs. For more information contact the publisher:

Published by Schiffer Publishing Ltd.
4880 Lower Valley Road
Atglen, PA 19310
Phone: (610) 593-1777; Fax: (610) 593-2002
E-mail: Info@schifferbooks.com

For the largest selection of fine reference books on this and related subjects, please visit our web site at **www.schifferbooks.com**
We are always looking for people to write books on new and related subjects. If you have an idea for a book please contact us at the above address.

This book may be purchased from the publisher.
Include $5.00 for shipping.
Please try your bookstore first.
You may write for a free catalog.

In Europe, Schiffer books are distributed by
Bushwood Books
6 Marksbury Ave.
Kew Gardens
Surrey TW9 4JF England
Phone: 44 (0) 20 8392 8585; Fax: 44 (0) 20 8392 9876
E-mail: info@bushwoodbooks.co.uk
Website: www.bushwoodbooks.co.uk

Library of Congress Control Number: 2010928426

Designed by RoS
Type set in Trajan Pro/Humanist 521 BT

ISBN: 978-0-7643-3562-4
Printed in China

Dedication

This book is dedicated to Bud & Elsie.

Contents

FOREWORD

The bowl is one of the most enduring items created by humans. Its origins can be traced back to the very earliest civilizations. There is no period in recorded history that was without the bowl and in many cultures today it is still preferred over the plate at mealtime. I consider the bowl to be quite noble in that, among other things, it is used to hold our food, the stuff of which we are made.

Until the twentieth century, wooden bowls were mostly of a utilitarian nature. Beginning in the 1930s, home workshops became more common and some turners began embellishing their creations. As the century progressed, all manner of decorative processes were applied to bowls. By the end of the century, they were painted, burned, carved, bleached, allowed to distort and crack, hammered, pierced, sandblasted, segmented, and embellished with silver, brass, and turquoise. All of these tortures were applied in the name of creating "art" from the common bowl. Some processes were more effective than others.

During this same period, a number of dedicated craftsmen began making "natural edge" bowls. Rather than produce a completely manmade object, they preferred to celebrate the life of the tree. By leaving that little bit of the tree's natural form in place, they were honoring its life, allowing the tree to show off just a bit of its former glory.

Bud Hohlfeld is an expert at bringing out the best in what a tree has to offer. Through this book you will learn the techniques he uses in turning natural edge bowls. These techniques are presented in a clear and concise manner with lots of pictures. With his guidance you can make your own creations to honor our stately friends, the trees.

William Smith
Gardenville, Pennsylvania

ACKNOWLEDGMENTS

Every time I watch someone turn wood I learn something, so I have to say thanks to all my fellow turners out there. However, there are some people who have influenced me at special times and in special ways. I would like to acknowledge them in chronological order. Dick Tuttle invited me to my first Keystone Turners Meeting and opened the door for me to a wonderful new world. John Perri took me under his big wing, showed me the basics, and encouraged me to continue. David Ellsworth sharpened my skills and pointed me in the direction of artistic turning. Cindy Drozda, through her work, compelled me to see better shapes in what I turn. And finally, Binh Pho, who inspires me to indulge my imagination and try for perfection. The combined influence of these five people, all great turners and great artists, have set me on a very happy and rewarding path. Thanks!

I also need to thank Amy, for her encouragement and support, and George and Judy Balock for all their help. And lastly I wish to thank Bill Smith for his generosity, encouragement and the wonderful foreword to this book.

Introduction

The physical act of turning wood and creating something that never existed before is intoxicating. We say a new enthusiast has been "bit by the turning bug." I had a wonderful reaction to the bite. In woodturning I have found an artistic outlet that uses all of my life experience. It is very satisfying. For me, the idea of a book on natural edge bowls has to include more than just the steps to accomplish the deed. So I have included some of my thoughts and philosophy on nature and shape. I hope that the instructions and illustrations on the following pages are encouraging to turners. To the readers who do not turn I hope this book enables them to see what is beautiful in the turnings they come across in their lives. Woodturning is considered a subtractive art. I hope this book adds to that.

NATURAL EDGE BOWLS

WHAT IS A NATURAL EDGE BOWL?

A natural edge Cherry bowl with straight grain and a regular curve on the edge.

This is a Norway Maple burl bowl with a very irregular natural edge.

A bowl that preserves the natural surface of the tree on its outer edge is a natural edge bowl. The bowl may or may not have the bark still attached. This is a simple definition. To a wood turner, a natural edge bowl is much more. A natural edge bowl is a collaboration or duet between the turner and the tree. The bowl blank becomes more than just raw material that is fashioned into the shape of a bowl with a regular rim giving up its identity to an imposed shape. The bowl blank maintains a sense of self through the turning process, and, with the help of the turning artist, becomes a thing of beauty, unique in the world.

When I turn a natural edge bowl, I am connecting with nature. The wood is an equal partner in the creative process and as I turn I realize what the potential is for that piece of wood. I look and listen and respond to the wood until we reach an accord. If I have done my part well, the completed piece will display the natural majesty previously hidden from view.

So what is a natural edge bowl? It is the beautiful, lasting result of a duet between man and nature.

Styles or Types of Natural Edge Bowls

A nice round Cherry log for a regular curve natural edge bowl.

Natural edge bowls fall into two basic categories: a. bowls with regular curvature on the edge and b. bowls with irregular edges.

As you can guess, a regular curve on the bowl edge will come from a round log. The more perfectly round the tree trunk is, the nicer the results. An irregular edge bowl can come from almost any part of the tree. One of the best sources for irregular shapes is the very base of the tree, the bottom 24". This part of the tree will usually have many buttresses and a great deal of figure in the grain due to compression. Burls also provide a great source of natural edge bowl stock.

The buttresses on this stump will yield bowls with wonderful figure.

A pile of burls and burl caps, both imported and domestic.

Grain Orientation

For a turner there are basically two ways to orient the grain of the wood while turning. In ***spindle orientation***, the grain of the wood to be turned is parallel with the bed of the lathe. In contrast, ***bowl orientation*** occurs when the grain is perpendicular to the bed of the lathe. Natural edge bowls can be turned either way. When turning a burl, the grain is so intertwined that these distinctions are meaningless.

This log is set up with a spindle orientation – with the grain.

This natural edge goblet was turned in spindle orientation.

This half Cherry log is set up in bowl orientation.

A natural edge Cherry bowl turned from a half log.

This Norway Maple burl is set up for a natural edge bowl. The grain swirls in all directions.

When I find a 12" to 14" diameter cherry log with straight grain, I automatically think of a natural edge bowl instead of a salad bowl. The best results you can hope for from a 14" log would be about a 12" salad bowl. If you create a natural edge bowl from the same log, you will be able to increase the finish diameter to the full diameter of the log and perhaps more.

This Cherry tree trunk has been cut to length and may yield ten natural edge bowls.

It is important when using round logs for natural edge bowls to center the annual growth rings in the bottom of the bowl. When completed, they should present the viewer with concentric ellipses in the bottom of the bowl. In order to do this, you should be a bit fussy in your selection of rough stock. Look for a nice, round log with regular, circular growth rings and the pith, the center of the first growth ring, in the center of the log. You can use a log that is oval, but be sure to cut it evenly on the long or short diameter. Remember, the growth rings should be centered on the center of the bowl. When you proceed this way, your end result will be a bowl with a nice, regular, natural edge that looks balanced.

When a log is round, the annual growth rings create a regular, concentric pattern inside the bowl.

Not all tree trunks grow with this regularity. This log will produce a beautiful pattern inside the bowl. All the rings form nearly perfect circles and the pith is centered in the log.

When you pick your stock carefully, you can have great results as this Cherry bowl illustrates.

The process is a little different for an irregularly shaped edge bowl. I talked about the "duet" between the artist/turner and the wood. As you are the animate one, you have to make all the decisions. Basically, you are trying to achieve some sort of balance between the shape and the surface. There is a lot to consider, such as the width or diameter, the height, and the curvature or shape of the bowl. I will provide more on this later. When you are out in the yard with your chain saw, you will need to make some basic decisions. Start by looking the wood over from all sides. If you are fortunate, you will see a shape in the wood that you find pleasing. Rough cut your bowl blank with the chain saw with the surface orientation in mind. You will want to try to balance what will be the resulting bowl edge. Try to avoid very low or very high sides. These will present problems on the lathe. Realize that you will be able to make some adjustments to the surface orientation when you set up for turning but you will want to keep this to a minimum.

This stump is over 3' across at the base and 2' high. What a find!

Look the wood over carefully before you make a cut and select the best features you can.

This roughed out blank should produce bowls with nice figure.

Additional Considerations

Burls and burl caps present a great range of opportunities. Some burls have a more or less regular domed shape and others do not. If you have a large burl or an entire tree that is covered in burls your choices are tremendous. In these situations, you can usually proceed as if you were working with a plain, irregularly shaped piece but add the additional consideration of the depth of the burl. Some burls are shallow. Elm burl, for example, can be relatively shallow compared to a maple burl. You want to turn a bowl that will display burl throughout and not disappear in the bottom. Also, when you are chain sawing out the rough blank, try not to cut too shallow and lose a portion of the figure.

This maple burl is nearly 3' in diameter. I paid $100 for this one. A bargain.

This is the burl from the previous illustration. It's a wonderful surprise to see that the burl goes so deep. I'm a lucky guy!

Burl caps, imported or domestic, will usually have a flat side where they were cut from the tree. This flat can be the top or bottom side of the bowl. Everyone is different so you have to consider this as well. Don't forget funky! I love symmetry, but sometimes a burl wants to be off center and asymmetrical. In the end these are your decisions as the artist; just remember it is a duet.

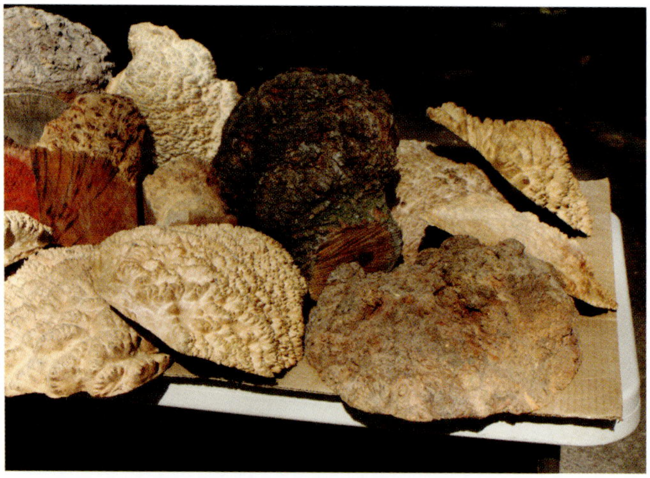

A pile of burl caps from around the world.

A Brown Mallee bowl turned a bit asymmetrical.

Preparing the Blank – Chain Sawing (Tools & Equipment)

Enough talk. Let's get out the chain saw. Don't forget the safety glasses, face shield, chaps, ear protection, gloves, and safety footwear. Make sure you have plenty of room to move around where you are working, and if you can, work with a buddy. Always follow safe cutting procedures and keep your chain sharp. This isn't a safety course and I won't be describing every procedure in depth. I intend to explain what to cut from the tree and not how.

Preparing the Blank for a Regular Curve Natural Edge Bowl

When you have selected your log, cut a section to the length you want. As an example, if you have a 14" diameter log and you want to make a salad bowl, you cut it to a little over 14". For a natural edge bowl you can cut it longer, 16" - 18". Split the log lengthwise on the pith. This will give you two bowl blanks. For a salad bowl, the opening of the bowl faces the center of the log, but for a natural edge bowl the opening faces the outside. If you can't turn the bowl right away, seal the open grain with green wood sealer or put the blank in a plastic bag. This will help keep the blank from drying and splitting until you can rough turn it.

Nice round Cherry log on the cutting block.

Split the log lengthwise on the pith to get two nice bowl blanks.

Two natural edge Cherry bowl blanks with wonderful grain.

If you can't turn the wood immediately, bag it in a plastic bag. This will prevent it from drying and cracking until you can get to it. Don't wait too long!

The rough bowl blank ready for trimming.

Preparing the Blank for an Irregular Natural Edge Bowl

Some good chain saw work at this point can save you a lot of extra work on the lathe. Once you have selected the surface you want for the top of the bowl try to locate the center of the bowl. I often use plywood discs with a hole drilled in the center to help layout the bowl size and center. This also helps me balance the surface. Rough cut the diameter for the bowl and cut a flat for the bottom that is parallel to the mean plane of the intended surface. Keep as much thickness as possible to add to your options for the proportions and shape of the bowl later.

A disc can help size the bowl and locate the center. Trace the perimeter with a marker and mark the center in the drilled hole of the disc.

Mark the cuts you want to make on the rough blank.

Trim the bottom parallel with the surface you want and keep it as thick as possible.

The trimmed blank does not need to be perfectly round but anything you can remove with the chain saw you won't have to remove with the gouge.

Rough Turning

Someone once said that if you gave fifty woodturners the same piece of wood you would get fifty different results. I agree! There are, however, generally two schools of thought on turning. One is to turn from green to finish and allow any change of shape due to drying to be reflected in the final piece. The other is to twice turn the object. The rough turning is done to give the bowl the general shape desired for the finished piece. The rough bowl is left thicker than the desired finish thickness. This is done to allow for the distortions and movement that will occur during the drying process. Use a moisture meter to check the moisture content of the bowl blank. Once it has dried to 12% moisture content or less, the bowl is returned to the lathe and turned to the finished size and shape, removing all distortion. I have done both but prefer to twice turn most bowls and hollow forms. As I said, I prefer symmetry.

Mounting & Orientation of the Bowl

There are several methods used to mount a bowl blank onto the lathe. Using a faceplate, using a screw center, and between centers are all good ways. They each have advantages and disadvantages.

Using a faceplate has the advantage of an excellent hold of the material. The disadvantages are being unable to mount onto the irregular surface of the natural edge bowl blank and the difficulty you will have threading the faceplate to the head stock thread on a large and heavy bowl. Additionally, mounting the faceplate to the base of the bowl blank will limit your ability to adjust the surface orientation for the edge.

A faceplate is screwed to the bottom of the bowl blank.

Screw centers fit into the chuck and are available in two lengths.

A screw center is a coarse, threaded adapter that fits into a four jaw chuck. A hole is bored in the center of the bowl blank face and this is spun onto the thread. The thread pulls the blank tight up against the jaws of the chuck. It is the most simple and easy way to mount a bowl blank, which is the greatest advantage. Disadvantages include that screw centers won't always grab well on soft or spalted wood and they also limit your ability to adjust the surface orientation of the bowl blank. You can make some modifications to the mounting procedure when using this method. For example, you can chisel or chop out a corrected area on the surface of the blank that will help change the orientation to something more desirable or you can use wedges to shift the orientation slightly.

Locate the center of the surface for the bowl.

Drill a 3/8" hole for the screw center.

This coarse threaded screw will pull the wood tight against the jaws of the chuck.

Shims used to help shift the orientation of the blank on the chuck jaws.

The major advantage of mounting between centers is the increased ability to change the surface orientation on the bowl blank. When you are trying to balance the shape with the edge of the bowl, this is very desirable. There are disadvantages, however. Try to imagine mounting a sixty-pound or larger wet bowl blank between centers. Even with a helper, it can be difficult. You also need a large drive center to handle big bowl blanks. Lastly, from a safety point of view, this method is the most risky. Natural edge bowl blanks do not always spin nicely. They wobble and can make your lathe walk across the floor if it isn't bolted down. This same imbalance can throw the blank right off the lathe if you turn the RPMs up too high, even on a small piece. But let me restate, the advantage is being able to make adjustments to the bowl orientation.

Maple burl bowl blank mounted between centers. Easier done with help!

A large drive center and a live tail stock center are a great help.

To begin between centers, locate the center of your top surface. I use two squares for this. Then transfer this location to the bottom. Use the squares again. Mark these centers with an awl so that you can find them more easily. Mount the bowl blank between the centers. Spin the blank by hand and use the tool rest as a reference. Balance the two opposite sides. Adjust the location of the top or drive center as needed until the opposite sides are approximately in the same plane. You may need to adjust this as you go, but this method helps to give you a very good rough start.

I use two squares and a rule to locate the center on the top surface.

Using the same squares helps to locate the center of the bowl on the bottom.

Once the bowl blank is mounted spin it by hand to make sure it won't hit your tool rest.

Using the tool rest as a reference, balance the opposite side of the bowl blank. The two low sides should be in line with each other and the higher sides with each other.

The reference marks used during the rough turning.

Shaping

Now that you have your bowl blank mounted securely on the lathe, you are ready to start shaping the outside. All you will need is a good bowl gouge and perhaps a parting tool to help true up a foot on the bottom of the bowl for the jaws of the chuck.

A well balanced bowl blank securely mounted and ready to turn.

A good bowl gouge is a necessity as well as a tool to form a square foot.
I use a 3/8" bedan.

Always start at the slowest speed!!!

Whether you are using a variable speed lathe or one on which you must physically change the belt speed, ***always start at the SLOWEST speed!*** Natural edge bowl blanks are always out of balance to start and will be thrown off your lathe if you start too fast. As with any other roughing procedure you must first remove all the high spots. When this is done, you will be able to turn up the speed a little. If the speed is turned up too high there will be vibration. A good speed is just under the speed where the vibration starts.

Here the tail stock center is shifted on the bottom of the bowl to re-orient the balance of the natural edge.

Changing, Finding Harmonious Balance

At this point you can refine the shape of the bowl to one that is pleasing to you. If you are working between centers, this is when you can adjust their locations to orient the edge of the bowl to what you want. If you are using a faceplate, you will not be able to make any changes while the bowl is attached to the faceplate. If you are using a screw center, you can try to shim the bowl and shift the bottom center slightly. Once you have shifted the centers to a new location, you must reshape the outside of the bowl again. When you have the shape you want, it is time to create a foot or tenon for the chuck jaws. Make sure the size is adequate for the size of the bowl and consider making the foot or tenon a bit oversized if you plan to core out several smaller bowls from the blank.

You can use shims to help change the orientation of the bowl edge when you use a screw center.

Make the tenon for the chuck large enough to support the bowl for coring. Make sure the shoulders of the tenon are square and made in solid wood.

What You Have vs. What You Want

The bowl blank now has a shape. Is it really the shape you want? Perhaps you have made the shape and proportions fit the general shape and proportions of the rough bowl blank. If you had an image of the final outcome when you cut the blank with your chain saw you may be close to what you originally wanted. Now is the time to reconsider. Do not let the proportions of the original bowl blank intimidate you. Feel empowered to change your mind. Make sure you are happy with the shape before you continue.

Plan B – The Wood Reveals Its Secrets, Good & Bad

Shaping a rough blank is an adventure of discovery. I am always excited to be the first human to see the inside of the tree. Usually there is great beauty revealed in the grain, figure, color, and burl clusters. Occasionally you will discover nasty things like stones, bullets, nails, cracks, and rotten branches just to name a few. These discoveries, good or bad, are really design opportunities. When you find something beautiful within the wood you should stop and consider how to use the shape of the bowl to display this beauty. I can't tell you what to do exactly, but I will say pause and consider your next step. When you find something undesirable it becomes an exercise in problem solving. If there is a hidden crack, you may need to abandon this bowl blank just for safety reasons. Get another blank and avoid running the risk of a blow-up at high speed. After all, this stuff grows on trees. It may be possible to remove stones and nails and continue, and sometimes you can work past a rotten branch. Based on what you find, you may be forced to change your original plan. Bark pockets and fissures in burls will usually make the bowl more interesting. You may want to reinforce these defects with epoxy or fill them with something complimentary to the design and color of your bowl. Knots present a special problem. If they have bark around them, they will most likely shrink and get loose or fall out during the drying process. I try to avoid these kinds of knots.

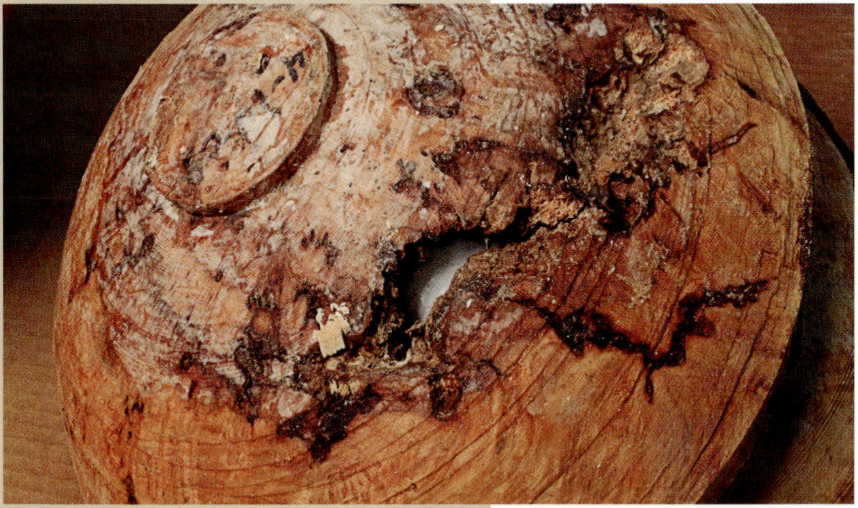

This is the type of defect, void, that can be filled with epoxy and the filling material of your choice to give the bowl a nice interior.

This crack is a defect that can be glued or reinforced with epoxy to give it strength and prevent it from blowing apart while you turn it. First turn the outside shape and apply the epoxy, then when you have your inside turned to its finish thickness, use the epoxy inside.

This type crack goes all the way to the edge and can blow apart. You must glue or epoxy this crack for safety.

Tall or Wide – Listen to the Wood

Listen with your eyes, not your ears. Look at the proportions of your bowl. The correct proportion should be pleasing to your eyes. You need to balance the size and proportions with the grain characteristics of the wood. For example, if most of the outer surface of a tall burl vase has burl markings but the bottom doesn't, the wood may be saying to you, "Please don't show my bottom." Perhaps you could take a bit more off that location and readjust the shape accordingly. So, if it is the outside of a tall vessel that is of most interest, it will be the inside of a wide vessel or bowl. Most bowls will be seen on a tabletop; you will be looking down on them. Your patrons will look at your work with the location that they want to place it in mind. Take a good look and listen!

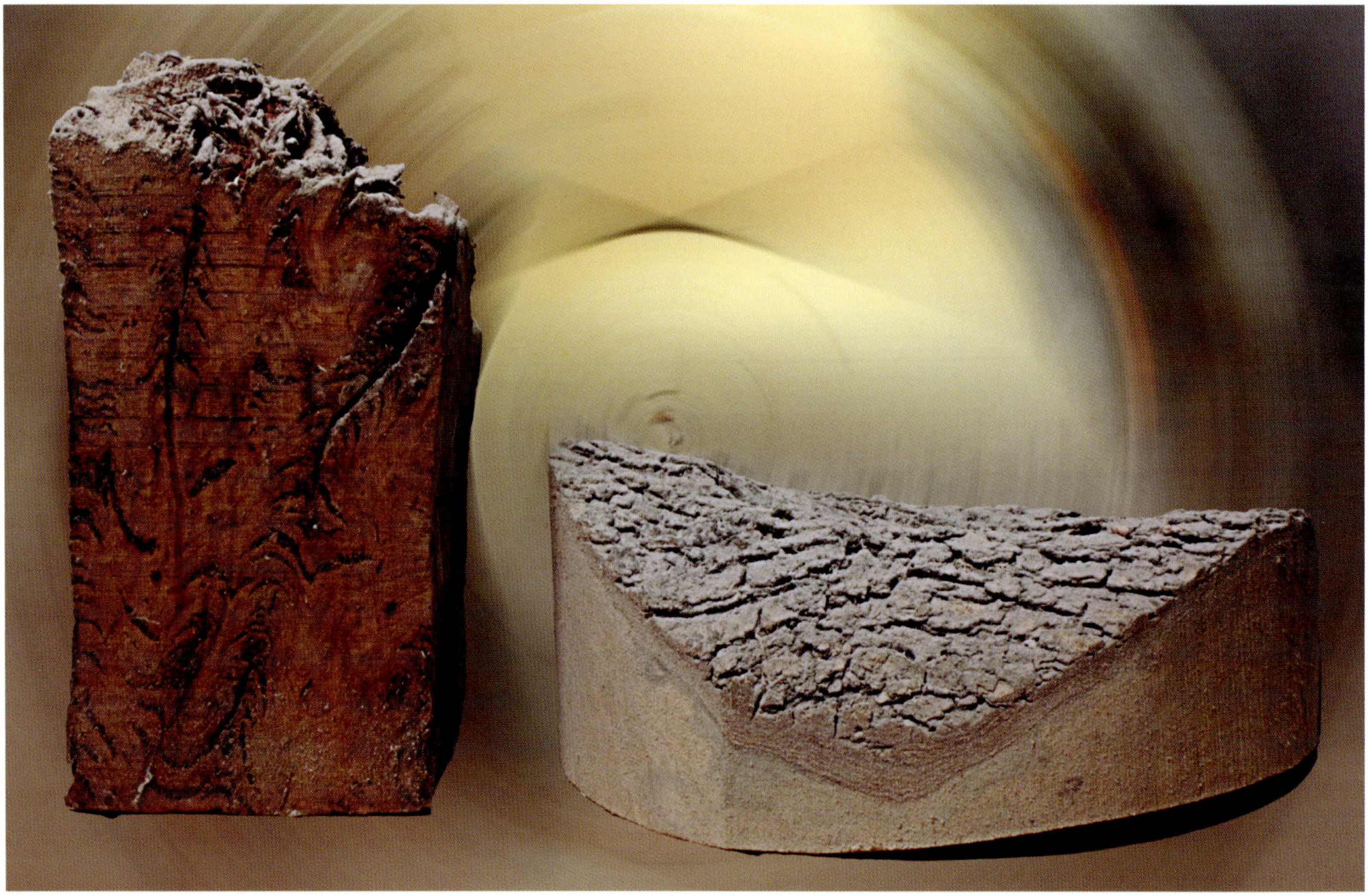

The rough turning stock you begin with can help you decide if the piece will be tall or wide!

Going All the Way the First Time or Drying

It sure is fun to turn green wood. I love turning green wood. Occasionally, I will turn something from green wood to finish in one session. Many turners do the same and find the results very satisfying. There is no denying that the results are interesting and somewhat unpredictable. The figure in the wood causes all sorts of distortion and on a natural edge vessel this can add to the character of the piece. When a burl or figured bowl is turned green to its finish surface, that surface will develop a texture due to the shrinkage of the wood cells. This can add to the tactile experience of the piece. Sometimes the distortion can turn a lovely shape into something less desirable. Beauty is in the eye of the beholder. It is, of course, your choice. I prefer to allow the rough turned bowl or hollow form to dry and then turn it a second time. I like the interchange of the smooth symmetrical surface of the curve with the natural interruption of the edge.

When you are turning the inside of a bowl, you will start in the center and work your way out to the edge, leaving the appropriate thickness for a second turning or your thickness of choice for a once and done. For a large bowl blank, or a special piece of wood, you may want to core out several bowls at this point.

This is a Norway Maple burl hollow form turned from green to finish in one session. It has retained its symmetry. Burls maintain their shape and distort somewhat less while drying than straight grained wood. Drying time is reduced when you turn the walls thin.

Unfortunately this thin Cherry burl turning has distorted to the point it lost its beautiful shape.

This twice turned Sassafras bowl shows a great interaction between the natural edge and shape.

Coring

Even though it grows on trees, beautiful wood is precious. When you have a lovely burl or figured piece of wood, consider using a coring system to create several bowls from that one bowl blank. There are many systems on the market. If it is not possible to acquire one of your own, borrow one, or take your bowl to a friend's shop and use his. You may be able to get three or more bowls from one 18" bowl blank. This not only helps to save wood and the environment but also can increase your income. After you core out a section, clean up the inside surface. True up the rough bowl to a uniform thickness, approximately 1" of thickness for every 10" of bowl diameter. The uniform thickness will help with even drying.

A figured piece of Silver Maple chucked up for coring.

Starting the coring cutter. Position the cutter to allow the correct wall thickness and depth.

After the initial depth is reached, the cutter must be removed and the cutter support arm inserted in the kerf. With the cutter supported, you may continue.

You may need to adjust the depth of the cutter and arm several times. Eventually you will get a rough bowl and another blank to use.

Clean up the wall thickness to a uniform thickness. This helps the blank to dry evenly.

Bark

Keeping the bark on the edge of your bowl isn't just due to luck. If you can get the wood very soon after the tree is cut down, and the bark is intact at that time, proper handling can help preserve the bark. There are, however, no guarantees. As soon as you can, you should rough turn the bowl blanks and coat them on the outside with green wood sealer. Also coat the inside edge of the bowl down an inch or two. This will slow down the drying process but it will also help prevent the outside of the bowl from developing cracks as well as helping to keep the bark from drying faster than the wood. When the wood sealer is dry, you can set the bowl blanks in the corner of your shop, on a shelf, in paper bags, or in a homemade wood drying kiln. Just don't put them in a drafty or windy place, any place that has great temperature changes like an attic, or in direct sunlight. When they have dried to about 12% moisture content or less they will be ready to finish turn. To be honest, I believe that it doesn't matter what you do to prevent bowls from cracking; if they want to they will.

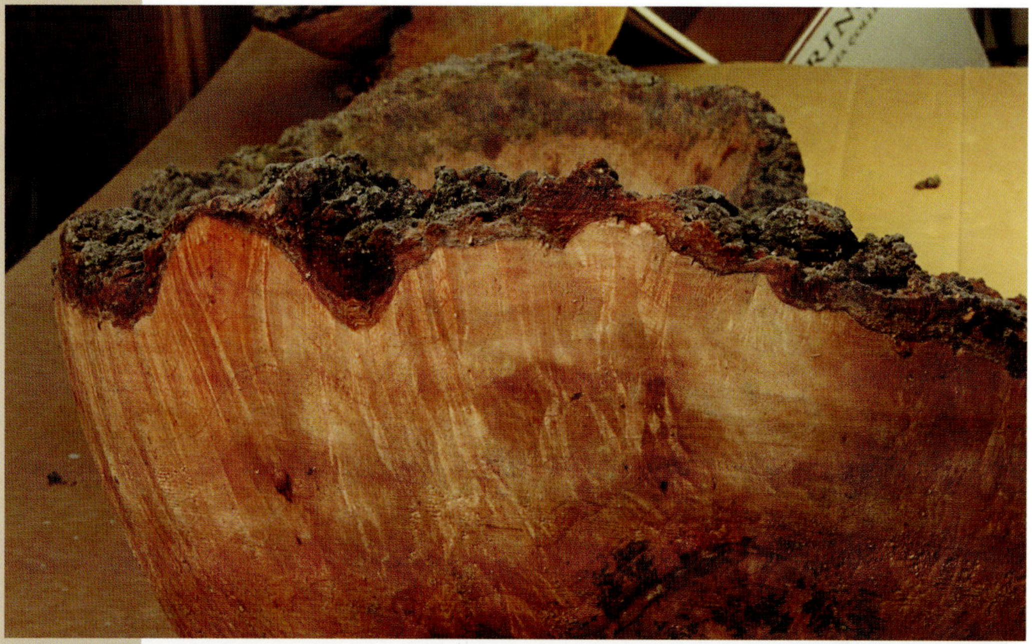

The bark on this dry Maple burl has remained attached during the drying process.

The bark on this Silver Maple popped off while drying.

Green wood sealer on the inside of the bowl edge.

Green wood sealer on the entire outside of the bowl.

My kiln is an old upright freezer. Only the shelves remain inside.

On the inside of the kiln is a 40w bulb in a socket in the bottom. Ventilation holes have been drilled in the bottom and top. Air inside is heated by the bulb. Moisture from the wood is removed as the hot air escapes out the top. Generally the drying time is reduced by 75%.

This bowl cracked badly while drying. Do not turn bowls like this; it's too risky. It's back to the burn pile with this one.

This piece cracked shortly after roughing the outside. It may be possible to return a foot and salvage something from it.

FINAL TURNING

Generally what happens to a rough turned bowl blank while it is drying is that it becomes oval. The wood shrinks more across the grain than it does with the grain, hence the oval shape. This is what happens to bowl blanks that are cut from regular or straight-grained logs. As a bowl blank from highly figured wood or a burl dries, all sorts of distortion can take place. In every case the bowl blank will no longer be round and before you can finish turning it you should true up the tenon for the chuck. Some form of a jamb chuck is required. A simple piece of rounded stock will work well but use something that is large enough to stabilize the bowl. Place the bowl over the jamb chuck and use a piece of foam rubber, rug-padding works well, between the bowl and the wood of the jamb stock. This will take up some irregularities and keep the two pieces of wood from slipping on each other. Bring the tailstock up and center it on the tenon. Secure it firmly. The bowl should not be loose. Always rotate the bowl by hand first to see if there are any problems. At this point you have an opportunity to adjust the orientation of the natural edge. If you think you need to make a small adjustment, you can relocate the tail center to a new location on the tenon and shift the bowl perhaps as much as an inch in a new direction. Your choice! Adjust the tool rest to reshape the tenon and start at the slowest speed. Bring the speed up to a point just below where there is vibration and make the necessary cuts to square up the tenon for the chuck. While the bowl is set up like this you can start to reshape the outside surface. Get the majority of the irregularities out but don't spend too much time with this step. When you re-chuck the new tenon, there may be some slight difference that you will need to re-cut to get the bowl running true. Once the bowl is back in the chuck, I like to take a few truing up cuts from the inside of the bowl before I go back to the outside surface. This helps to reduce the vibration from the irregularities on the inside of the bowl.

During drying this Walnut blank went oval. It is 1/2" smaller across the width. That is why we make the rough blank bigger.

The tenon for the chuck on this bowl is oval after drying and should be trued up before it is put in the chuck.

This jamb chuck is used to help remount bowls for their second turning.

A piece of foam carpet padding is used as a cushion between the bowl and the jamb chuck.

The jamb chuck, padding, and bowl in place.

Bring the tail stock live center up to secure the bowl in place.

Reshape and square up the tenon.

Begin to reshape the outside of the bowl while it is on the jamb chuck.

Here you can see how the bowl has gone out of round.

Completely reshape the outside of the bowl while it is on the jamb chuck. You will need to clean it up a bit more once it is in the jaws of the chuck, so don't get too fussy at this point.

I like to take a few truing cuts on the inside of the bowl once it is in the chuck.

Cleaning up the inside of the bowl will help reduce vibration and make the final cuts on the outside easier to do.

Be sure the bowl is seated well against the jaws of the chuck. Shape the outside of the bowl to the lovely shape you have in mind. If there is a bit of irregularity in the surface, you will need to true it up again. Make your final shaping cuts. Keep your gouge sharp and take light cuts. Try to eliminate all your tool marks. Make sure your bowl gouge is freshly sharpened and use a shear scraping technique on the final passes. The outside should be ready for sanding.

When the inside is roughed out and the outside is running true, use a shear scraping cut with your gouge to clean off the tool marks.

The gouge is held at a 45 degree angle and guided up and across the surface of the bowl. Take light cuts.

Shear scraping greatly improves the quality of the surface and reduces sanding time. Shear scrape as much of the outside as you can. You won't be able to get at the bottom easily, but you can finish that later.

If you have done a good job of rough turning, the wall thickness of your bowl should be somewhat uniform. If it is not, try to correct this now. A uniform thickness will assist you in turning the inside. You must consider what you want for a final thickness at this point. Making a bowl very thin just because you have the skill may not compliment the overall size and shape of the bowl. Also, the edge itself has a presence that should be presented properly. Bark on thin bowls will break off very easily from handling by your customers. If there is no bark on this natural edge, think about possibly texturing the edge. If you decide to texture the edge, there should be some thickness on which to work. I am not saying to avoid turning thin bowls. I am saying consider all of the characteristics of each individual bowl and work with them. Listen to the wood!

Start to remove material from the inside of the bowl in stages, 1" to 2" at a time.

Now that you have made your decision, set up your tool rest to begin. Use a very light cut on the initial pass. Try to take the first cut down to a point that is below the lowest part of the edge. Establish your final thickness before you proceed deeper. Follow the outside contour of the bowl. Continue in increments of one to two inches. Try not to go back to the edge and re-cut. By the time you are half way down the interior curve the outer edge will start to distort. If you try to re-cut the edge you will likely have a catch and destroy the bowl. Take your time, keep your gouge sharp, and blend each section as you go. Having a uniform thickness before you start will help you gauge the amount of wood you are removing as you cut each section. For example, if the uniform rough thickness is about 3/4" and you want a finish thickness of 3/8" you will be removing 3/8" in several passes. So, keeping an eye on the amount of material you remove from the inside will reassure you that you are where you want to be. Still, check the thickness with calipers as you go. I will often use a large, round nose scraper to blend each section and to complete the curve of the bowl bottom. Now it is ready for sanding.

Work the first cuts down to a point that is below the natural edge.

Decide on a wall thickness that fits the proportions of the bowl. Remember to consider the character of the edge. Make it as thick or thin as you feel is complimentary to the overall appearance of the bowl.

Continue to remove the material in stages and blend the stages as you go. Use a large round nose scraper if necessary. Try not to re-cut the rim area as it will most likely be a bit out of round at this point and a nasty catch can ruin all your nice work.

Here is the bowl, ready for sanding.

I do very little hand sanding on bowls. I use 3" sanding discs and a close quarters drill. Start with as coarse a grit as you need, 80 or 100, and finish with 320 or 400. You can continue to a finer grit if you like. I have sanded up to 4000 on some pieces. It depends on the results you want.

I power sand with a close quarters drill with a foam sanding pad. I start with 80 or 100 grit and work my way up to 320 or 400. I sand inside and outside at this time. I spin the bowl both forward and in reverse. Don't forget to use dust collection and wear a facemask.

This transfer adapter is an indispensable gadget. It mounts on the tail stock live center.

Finishing off the foot of the bowl is also a decision-making process. To complete the bottom, I remove the bowl and the chuck from the headstock and use a transfer adapter to center the bowl on my vacuum chuck. If you do not have a vacuum chuck, you will remove the bowl from the chuck and mount it back on the jamb chuck, bringing the tailstock up to the center again and seat it firmly. Set up the tool rest and shape the foot. You may want a large foot, a small foot, a foot you can carve, or no foot at all. Your choice, but again consider how the foot will work with the bowl's shape. Finish sand the bottom. You may want to decorate the bottom or leave it simple. If you are using a vacuum chuck, just remove the tailstock and finish the bottom. Add your own personal touch, if you like. If you are using a jamb chuck, it is a bit trickier. Finish off as much of the bottom as you can or as you feel safe doing. You will have to carve or sand off the stub that remains after you remove the bowl. Always undercut the bottom slightly to allow the bowl to seat well on a flat surface.

Remove the chuck with the bowl in it and transfer it to the adapter. This will center the bowl on the bell of the vacuum chuck.

Bring the tail stock up to secure the bowl.

Finish off the bottom and create the foot you want. Sand this area as well.

I like to decorate the under part of the foot and create a place to sign the bowl.

If you do not have a vacuum chuck, remount the bowl using the jamb chuck and tail stock. Turn the foot to the shape you want, leaving a small stub to keep the bowl secure. Make this stub as small as you feel still gives you security. Sand the bottom, remove the bowl, carve off the stub, and you are done.

Important note, always undercut the bottom a bit to prevent the bowl from rocking when it is on a flat surface.

The Perfect Curve

So what does the perfect curve look like? This is a matter of opinion, so here is mine. The curve on a bowl should be flowing, balanced, and uninterrupted. The curve may change direction but the separate curves created should always be in proportion. If possible, on a natural edge bowl, the curve(s) should enhance the interaction with the edge, not interfere with it.

The finished bowl with a lovely, flowing, uninterrupted parabolic curve.

This bowl exemplifies a beautiful natural curve that is in harmony with the shape of the natural edge.

"Perriesque."

Perriesque

My good friend and teacher, John Perri, helped me to see the visually pleasing shape of a parabolic curve in the shape of a bowl. John made beautiful bowls with wonderful curves and I now use the term "Perriesque" in homage to him. The parabola is a natural regular curve. The proportions of the curve may vary but it is important that visually the curve be uninterrupted. Your eyes must be able to follow the curve without distraction. Things like sudden changes in direction or flat spots will spoil the experience. Curves may also be combined to create a lovely shape. A positive and negative curve creates an "S" shape or what we call an Ogee shape. On this type of combined curve the proportions of the two curves are important. They do not need to be the same size but they need to balance each other. An Ogee curve will not easily lend itself to a natural edge bowl. You will need to find the right combination of proportion and surface in the wood you choose.

The small change in direction on the curve of this Maple burl bowl enhances the overall appearance.

The regular curve of the straight grained natural edge Cherry bowl works well with the overall shape of the bowl.

The Perfect Bottom

This is an ongoing debate. Some opine there is no need for a bottom. Some state that the bottom is like a pedestal that should display the bowl. My opinion is that everyone is correct. Sometimes there is no need for a bottom. A rocking bowl adds the kinetic aspect. Of course this should be done deliberately. A fruit bowl might be better with a stable bottom. A large pedestal base on a bowl can really display that bowl to great advantage as long as the bowl is being displayed and not the pedestal. There is need for harmony here. The base should not detract from the bowl and the bowl should not overpower the base. On a functional bowl, such as a salad bowl, nut bowl, etc., the base should be functionally supportive. If it is too small or high, the bowl will be unstable and its contents may escape at an embarrassing moment.

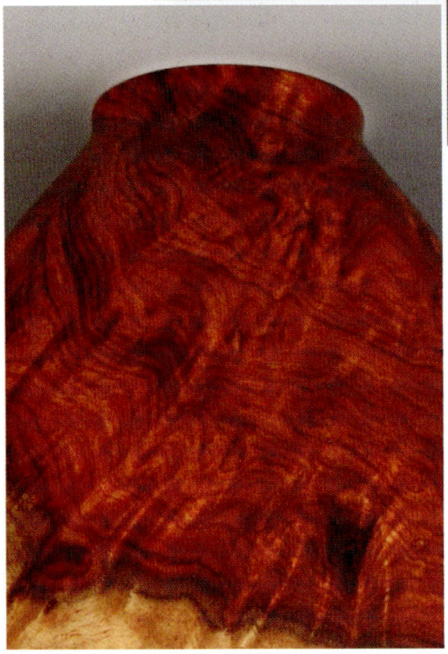

Thick or Thin – Listen to the Wood

We have all heard the phrase, "Thin to win." Thin, light bowls are very appealing. They display the turner's skill. However, turning a bowl thin without regard to the proportions of the overall piece can be a mistake. A large bowl that is too thin may break easily when handled and thin bowls are rarely functional. Everyday use will quickly take a toll on a very thin bowl. Many people are reluctant to handle a very thin turning and won't make that purchase. Light, thin, delicate turnings can be very beautiful simply because of those characteristics. Thick bowls are usually heavy in the hand. If a very large bowl has thick walls, it can be difficult for some folks to lift. Large, beautifully shaped pieces make bold statements. By now I think you will realize that I advocate balance and proportion. The wall thickness should vary and work with the overall appearance, enhancing not detracting. When you look at a bowl you may hear a little voice in the back of your mind say, "Nice bowl, but the edge is a bit thick/too thin." So when you turn that bowl you need to ask as you turn, "Are the edges too thick?" and "Are the edges thin enough now?"

This delicate hollow form is turned to 3/32". The rim thickness and the burl lines complement each other.

This bowl is turned to about a 3/16" wall thickness. The edge has nearly regular undulations that work well with the grain pattern. All provided by nature.

This bowl has a relatively thick edge, but the character of the edge adds a great deal that would be lost if it were turned too thin.

On Beyond Turning

I could create an endless list of tools and equipment used to augment your completed turning. There are catalogs full of them. In order to focus this discussion, I will divide it into the following categories: edge & surface treatments, burning, carving, piercing, and finishing.

Edge & Surface Treatments

The natural edge on this bowl was brushed with a wire wheel to create a striated texture.

This Silver Maple bowl was very near rotten. Sand blasting the surface was a way of texturing that made the bowl much more interesting.

This is "Old King's Bowl." Sand blasted and bleached, it looks old, like something found on the beach.

The first and most obvious surface treatment is smooth sanding. You may decide that is all there needs to be. If you wish to further augment your work, a good start is a smooth surface. I should say here that a rough turned surface that uses the tool markings as a texture is a legitimate treatment. It is possible that you may only want to embellish the natural edge of the bowl. Texturing the edge with a dimple pattern or a wire brush are two easy ways to add something extra. Whatever you want to try, I strongly suggest that you work out the process on a piece of similar scrap material before you go to the finished piece. It is worth the time to do this.

If you want to decorate the surface of your bowl either partially or completely, you should again work out the process on a similar piece of scrap material. Some techniques that yield interesting surface results are sand blasting and brushing with a wire wheel. Both remove the softer portion of the annual growth rings and enhance that pattern in the surface. Sandblasting also works on spalted or punky wood to give it an aged or weatherworn appearance. A repetitive impact or percussion pattern also brings new character to the piece. Experiment with different types of tips in a reciprocating carver to get the desired results.

BURNING

Years ago when I first started, a friend made the comment that my show and tell piece might look better if it was burned. I thought for a moment and, since I am not paranoid, said what do you mean? Taking a propane torch to the surface of some woods, ash in particular, will blacken the surface and burn out some of the softer parts of the annual growth rings. Wire brushing or sand blasting after can create a beautiful effect. Sometimes simply burning the natural edge of a piece will add to the final appearance. Burning also means pyrography. Using various wood burning hand pieces can create different decorations or surface textures.

The edge of this small bleached bowl was burned with a butane torch to add a bit of contrast.

The surface of this small form has a pattern that loosely follows the grain lines. The pattern and edge were burned in with pyrography tools.

The edge of this spalted Ash bowl was wire brushed and then burned with a small butane torch.

Carving

Carving probably has the broadest range of possibilities. Hand carving or power carving the edge or surface of the finish turned form can change it completely. Keep in mind that we are talking about natural edge forms so the pattern or subject matter of the carving should enhance, not detract, from the piece.

Sometimes the carving can be done on the lathe with the wood spinning. This is really a form of texturing.

The surface of this natural edge hollow form has been relief carved along the grain lines.

PIERCING

In order to create beautiful pierced work, the form needs to be turned thin. Very thin! To pierce a pattern or decoration through a turning, the wall thickness should be 1/16" to 3/32". A pierced wall allows the observer to see through to the inside. This brings the characteristic of the inside into play with the outside. The combination can be quite striking or interruptive. I try to compliment the contour of the edge by using a band of piercing that follows the general undulations that form the edge. I try not to be rigid about this. If the edge is flowing, I allow some latitude in the band of piercing. It doesn't have to be an even width. I also prefer to use a random piercing pattern on natural edge pieces; however, I am not rigid about that either. A natural edge bowl displays an air of freedom, so any decorative piercing should support, maintain, or enhance that freedom.

The pierced pattern on this bowl brings the inside color to the surface.

When I pierce a decorative band around the rim of a natural edge bowl, I generally follow the shape of the edge.

This natural edge Sycamore bowl has a free form piercing.

Finishing

There are so many good finishes on the market that I really can't say what you should use to do the job. Use what you are familiar with. There are a few considerations when you choose a finish, however. Usually, the first thing to consider is if the bowl will be used for food. If you have planned to make a bowl for use with food, you must use a finish that is food safe and will stand up to that use. Lacquers and acrylics are really not suitable for functional bowls. A simple mixture of mineral oil and beeswax is a standard for functional bowls. This finish will not produce a high shine or luster. If you wish to produce a glossier finish, you will need to use a good quality food safe varnish. Use as many coats as are needed to produce the desired results. You may wish to use a buffing system to complete the job. I use two or more coats of Tung Oil varnish. I simply wipe it on with a clean cotton cloth and let it dry for several days between coats. I also use #0000 steel wool between coats to smooth the surface. After the final coat, I steel wool the surface once again and then buff the entire bowl with Tripoli and apply Carnauba wax with a buffing wheel. This creates a softer sheen.

For artistic turnings, pieces not intended for use with food, I usually use a clear acrylic. I have found that the acrylic finishes can be buffed out with more success than lacquer finishes. But use whatever works for you.

Here is our figured Silver Maple bowl ready to be finished.

A simple block with three nails is used to support the bowl while the finish is drying.

Necessary equipment is the bowl, a clean cotton cloth, rubber gloves, and Tung oil varnish.

The first coat of finish will begin to bring out the color and grain. Between coats use #0000 steel wool on the surface. Several coats may be necessary to achieve the finish you want.

Cotton buffing wheels are used on the surface of the bowl. I use Tripoli compound on one wheel and Carnauba wax on the other. I rarely use white diamond compound.

These ball buffs are great for the inside of smaller bowls.

Here is the finished product.

What a transition! Tree stump to tabletop!

MATERIALS

WHERE DO YOU GET THIS STUFF?

I have been asked more times than I can count, "Where do you get this stuff?" Trees grow all over the world, so that's the answer. You may live in "Wood Heaven," the eastern mountain range states of the U.S., or some other forested area. Unless you live in the desert, there should be something to turn nearby. Burls grow on just about every deciduous tree. Most trees will branch, which forms crotches. Beautiful figured wood comes from the stressed parts of the tree, like the base or under heavy branches. So you have choices. You can invest in a chain saw and some equipment and learn how to harvest your own stock, or you can purchase stock from someone else. I do both. I will not cut down a tree for the wood to turn a bowl but if the tree is going to be cut down for other reasons I'll try to contact the owner and make a deal. I usually offer a bowl for some wood, which can work for both parties. Tree surgeons are a good source. I have found they can be generous or may sometimes charge a small fee, and very often will work with you to help you get what you want. Ask them about burls!

Burls, Domestic and Imported

Domestic burls are just as beautiful as imported burls. Now that I've said that, I have to admit that the colors of some of the imported Australian burls are irresistible. I have spent lots of money on them but have never been disappointed. If you can't find burls from a local source where you can see them before you buy them, then you can shop on the Internet. When you shop on the Internet, try to work with a place that has good photos of the stock and a size reference of some sort. Shop around; there are a lot of suppliers. Also ask other turners where they get their stock. Most of the stock from Australia is in the form of burl caps. Burls are harvested from the tree and the tree produces more. Domestic burls are mostly from trees that have been cut down. There are also root burls. Some species, such as California Buckeye, will form a burl in the ground. Root burls are great; however, they may have some ingrown stones or dirt that will cause you some problems. If you really want to turn burls, you will find them.

Even without burls you can turn beautiful natural edge bowls from just about any log. The concentric straight grain round log is a great place to start.

Natural Edge Hollow Forms

A bowl is really just an open hollow form. Turning hollow forms is not our topic here, so I won't go into the process of how they are created. I will say again, you need to try for a balance between the top and the rest of the form. A top that is too large can dominate a small form and should be avoided. A small top on a large vessel will also be out of place.

Have fun, listen to the wood, and play your duet!

GALLERY

This gallery contains pictures of my natural edge work from the last five years. It is not all my natural edge work, but it is a fair representation of what I have done. The pieces are not grouped chronologically, but start with simple straight grain work and proceed to the more complicated. I hope you enjoy them.

OF NATURAL EDGE TURNINGS

Spalted Oak bowl, 9" x 4", turned in David Ellsworth's class.

Cherry Bowl, 16" x 6".

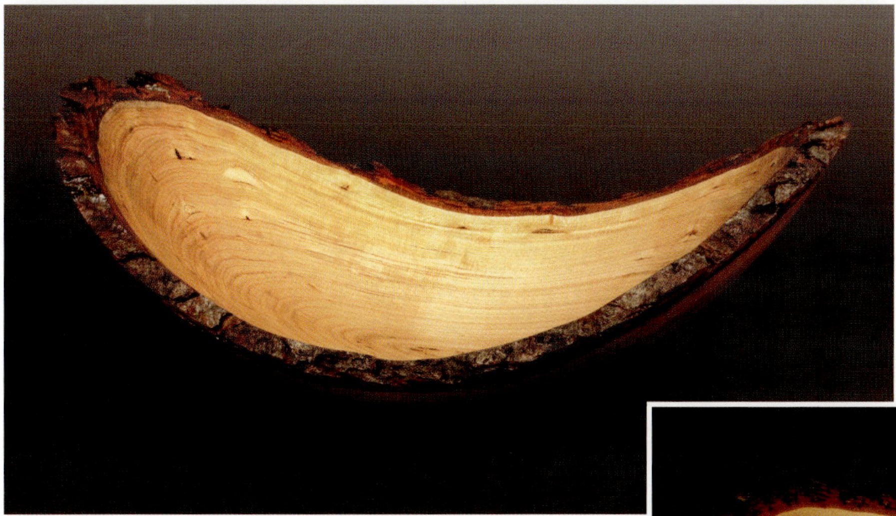

Cherry Bowl, 15" x 4".

Cherry Bowl, 10" x 4".

Cherry Bowl, 16" x 5".

Sycamore Bowl, 11" x 6".

Sycamore Bowl, 10" x 5".

Cherry Bowl, 12" x 5".

Cherry Bowl, 10" x 4".

English Walnut Bowl, 17" x 5".

Spalted Ambrosia Maple Bowl, 11" x 5".

Nicely Spalted Maple Bowl, 9" x 5".

Maple Burl Bowl, 11" x 3".

Spalted Ambrosia Maple Bowl, 9" x 4".

Spalted Ambrosia Maple Bowl, 10" x 5". I've kept this one.

When I turned this 12" x 7" Sassafras bowl, it filled the shop with aroma!

"Dahling, How Did Yew Get So Thin?" Yew is wonderful to turn. This 8" x 7" bowl shows the lovely color.

Maple Burl Bowl, 8" x 6".

Ambrosia Maple Bowl, 10" x 4", turned thin then bleached and finished with semi-gloss acrylic.

A wonderful 14" x 6" Maple Burl bowl from a tree in Blue Bell, PA.

Another aromatic adventure with Sassafras. 9" x 8" bowl, I wish I had more!

"Dahling, How Did Yew Get So Thin Too?" This is the other part of the log my friend George gave me.

Norway Maple Burl, 19" x 8". This came from "The Tree" from New Holland, PA. The entire tree was burl.

This bowl was cored out from the bowl of the previously shown Norway Maple Burl. It is 14" x 5".

This 12" x 3" bowl also came from a tree in Blue Bell, PA.

"Serendipity." I found a nice chunk of Maple Burl under a shelf in my workshop. It was in a plastic bag and lost for five years. It was dry and the colors a bit grey, but it made a lovely 9" x 7" bowl.

The shape of this 9" x 8" Maple Burl bowl is quite like what my friend John Perri would turn. John would probably make the foot a bit smaller.

This 7" x 7" bowl was turned from a cut-off chunk from "The Tree."

This 6" x 3" piece was turned from spalted Maple, bleached, and finished with a matte acrylic spray.

Australian Burl caps come in all sizes. This is a Red Mallee bowl, 13" x 2".

This 12" x 2" Horistes Burl is also from Australia.

This small Red Mallee bowl, 6" x 1", was cored from a larger piece.

This Big Leaf Maple burl came from Oregon. It made a nice 8" x 4" bowl.

This 6" x 7" Black Walnut vase actually came from the crotch of a tree from Lancaster, PA, that was blown down in a storm.

Almost a hollow form, this little bowl has a lot of character. 7" x 5" red Maple burl.

A Red Morrel burl also from Australia, very colorful. 12" x 2". As you can see, many of the Australian burl caps are not very thick.

Yellow Box Burl has such lovely color. This beauty is 14" x 3".

This is a Tasmanian Eucalyptus Burl bowl. I call this form a turned over edge. 9" x 3".

This burl cap was sold as a "Goldfield" burl. It was so lovely it sold within the first hour of showing. 14" x 2".

Brown Mallee is one of my favorite Australian burls. This one is 11" across the wings and 2" deep.

This is a little chunk of Oak burl, which made a semi-hollow form. 5" x 2".

This is another Tasmanian Eucalyptus Burl bowl. 8" x 3".

This red Mallee was a bit pale but the grain and edge were enough. 7" x 2".

9" x 2" Red Mallee bowl.

Beautiful deep color on this small Red Mallee bowl, 7" x 2".

This was one of the nicest Red Mallee burl caps I've turned to date. 15" x 3".

Another Red Morrel burl cap bowl, 10" x 2".

Corrugata Burl bowl, 13" x 3". I was listening, so I just let the burl do all the talking.

Brown Mallee bowl, 7" x 2".

Brown Mallee bowl, 8" x 2".

Brown Mallee bowl, 9" x 2".

A Norway Maple burl bowl from "The Tree." 10" x 4".

A Norway Maple burl bowl from "The Tree." 11" x 3".

A Norway Maple burl bowl from "The Tree" – just 5" x 5", but with great presence. Don't throw away those little cut-offs.

A Norway Maple burl bowl from "The Tree." 10" x 4".

Another little beauty from "The Tree;" however, the bark came off. I'm still a lucky guy! 4" x 5".

Another oblate spheroid, 9" x 6", turned green to finish.

"Black Pui Pot." It is actually made from a Black Pui log. I used the whole log. The sapwood and heartwood make a great contrast. 8" x 8".

A natural edge hollow form of bleached Silver Maple. Oblate spheroid, 9" x 6".

My daughter and son-in-law were hiking and found an Eastern Hornbeam burl that became this little hollow form, 5" x 5".

"Morgan." This little 6" x 5" hollow form came from a tree from Morgantown, PA.

Amboyna Burl, expensive stuff but so beautiful. This 4" x 7" vase sold within fifteen minutes of the show opening. Not surprising.

Spalted Maple Burl vase, 6" x 9".

Beautiful Jarrah Burl. My friend Anna bought this 5" x 7" vase as a gift.

This Aromatic Red Cedar vase is turned on the pith. I cheated a little for the natural edge part. The log was sawn off at an angle and when I turned it the fissures on the edge created this pattern. I haven't been able to recreate this. 5" x 10".

Natural edge top hollow form of Maple Burl, 7" x 10".

Natural edge opening hollow form of Maple Burl, 7" x 4".

A small natural edge top Elm Burl hollow form, 6" x 5".

A small natural edge top hollow form of Maple Burl, 5" x 8".

"Desert Water." Silver Maple hollow form that is relief carved on the annual growth rings, bleached, painted, and finished with matte acrylic. 8" x 5".

"Serendipity II." There were actually two forgotten burl blanks under my shelf. The hard part here was hollowing out this DRY maple burl. 10" x 11".

Natural edge opening hollow form of Norway Maple Burl from "The Tree." It was turned green to finish in one session. Great contrast between the heartwood and sapwood, 7" x 8".

"East Wind." 10" x 6", turned from Japanese Maple, green to finish in one turning.

"A Bradford Pearing." This small piece of Bradford Pear wood is also relief carved on the growth rings. The inside is painted as well as the underside of each carved ring. 5" x 4".

"Ort." Just a little leftover piece of maple that has decorative burn lines following the annual growth rings. The inside is airbrushed lightly. 7" x 5".

"Old King's Bowl." This spalted Silver Maple bowl was so punky I couldn't get a good cut on the surface so I decided to sand blast it and then bleach it. 13" x 7".

A natural edge Cherry bowl that lost its bark. I pierced a pattern along the edge. 9" x 4".

This thin Sycamore bowl is pierced with a random design that is almost unrelated to the natural edge and painted. 8" x 5".

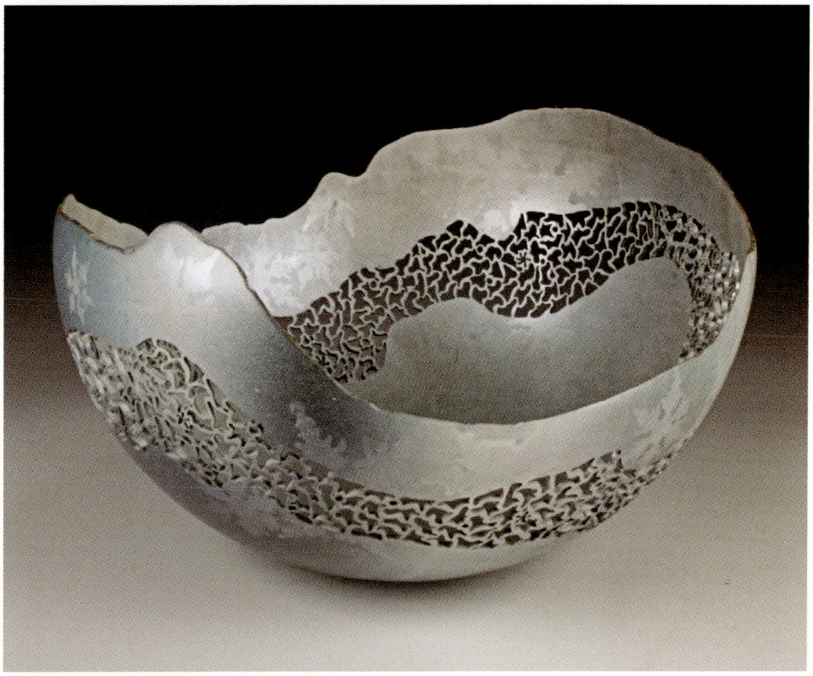

"Winter Bowl." Sycamore again, this time pierced with a band that roughly follows the edge. Snowflakes of interference paint cover the entire surface inside and out. 9" x 5".

The idea here is similar to the previous bowl; however, I painted the inside and outside of this Sycamore bowl with two very contrasting colors. The piercing brings the inside out and the outside in. 7" x 3".

"Spring Vase." I had to make a spring vase after the winter bowl so what better to use than daffodils. 5" x 6", pierced and painted maple with acrylic airbrush paints.

"Summer Bowl." We have four seasons here in the East, so eventually there will be Autumn Bowl, but the summer bowl had to have Tiger Lilies. Pierced and painted Bahamian Strong Bark wood, 8" x 6".

"Sea Through Bowl." I turned this thin Sycamore natural edge bowl and looked at it for six months before I saw the fan coral, everything else fell into place after that. I did alter the edge a bit for this one. 11" x 6".